PRO CODER'S GUIDE TO AI

CONQUERING THE AI REVOLUTION

PRO CODER SERIES

GREG L. TURNQUIST

MOUNTAIN
SUMMIT PRESS

CONTENTS

This book is dedicated to those who have followed me through thick and thin and still read my content. Your support has time and again strengthened me to continue writing, even when it is really hard to put pen to paper (or perhaps finger to keyboard!)

FOREWORD

When I think back to 2020, a period comes to mind that many of us would prefer to forget. The global pandemic consumed our lives that year. Yet amid those challenging times, something significant emerged: the first version of ChatGPT was released to the public in November 2020. As soon as I started using it I knew that this technology was going to change the future of work.

Since then, AI has transformed the world of software development and entered the mainstream. As developers, we've witnessed AI coding tools dramatically enhance our productivity through three key implementations: AI assistants, inline IDE assistants, and the emerging agentic AI IDEs. These powerful tools not only boost productivity but also help developers read and write code more efficiently, generate comprehensive documentation, and serve as valuable facilitators for continuous learning and skill development.

While developers across all skill levels have questioned their future role in the AI era, I maintain an optimistic perspective. I view generative AI in its current form as simply another powerful tool in our developer toolbelt, not a replacement. The critical factor is determining when and how to effectively leverage this technology for specific tasks. You cannot simply issue a basic prompt to AI and expect it to complete your work independently. This relationship represents a true collaboration where you remain the pilot, not merely a passenger. Rigorous code review remains essential, as blindly accepting machine generated solutions without careful evaluation contradicts the fundamental principles of quality software development.

Before Greg and I ever met, I was already a big fan of his work. I had read several of his books, including "Learning Spring Boot 2," and was immediately impressed. Greg possesses a remarkable ability to break down complex topics and present them in an accessible, understandable manner. In December 2020, Greg and I connected on a Zoom call for the first time. We discussed YouTube strategies, giving me the opportunity to reciprocate for all the knowledge he had bestowed upon me through his work. What struck me most about Greg was his genuine passion for learning, teaching, and contributing to the community. Greg and I were fortunate enough to later work together at VMware, where we collaborated on several projects that combined our complementary skills and shared enthusiasm for technology.

If you're reading this you already know the importance of AI for developers. This book provides essential foundations for integrating AI into your development workflow, starting with the fundamentals. Greg excels at transforming complex concepts into practical applications. What truly distinguishes this book is its focus on implementation rather than theory alone. Through topics like prompt engineering, Greg provides concrete, real-world guidance that you can apply immediately.

Happy Coding,

—Dan Vega
*Java Champion, Spring Developer Advocate, YouTuber, and
Lifelong Learner*

Over the past two years, a new tool emerged that I didn't know what to do with—ChatGPT.

I slowly dipped my toe in the water and then moved on to other stuff.

But I came back. This time I took two steps.

And again, I stepped back out and moved on.

I kept coming back. Multiple times. Each time, going a little further. Just a little bit more.

And then suddenly, I noticed that I had grabbed a small boat, climbed in, and was paddling.

I was kind of surprised!

The farther I went, the more my awareness of what I had discovered came into focus.

I had found something that was more revolutionary, more game-changing than anything I'd seen since I'd launched my career.

Suddenly, memories came to me. Like the time I took an Uber from Palo Alto to San Francisco. Every billboard I passed was for a different AI startup company. Other people were well aware that something was coming.

Everyone seems to be trying to capture this spark in their own bottle.

I don't know what will happen, let alone where we will all be in the next five or ten years.

But I suddenly knew that what I had learned and was in the thick of, I wanted to capture it and share it with you.

Because if you don't dip your toe in, grab your own boat, and start paddling, you're going to miss it.

I don't know what your future is or what role AI tools may play in it. But I want to get warmed up on it so you can at least make your own decisions about using it. Use it at all? A little? A lot? Only as an aid? Or for whole volumes?

I like to tell others that I have some pretty strong opinions on certain topics. AI is one such arena.

I want you to gain awareness of what's available and what's at stake. Then you'll be in a position to make such a decision for yourself.

—Greg

1 / GETTING STARTED WITH AI

Rarely do we have the chance to witness something as grand as the Industrial Revolution. Because that is what we're in the midst of.

The AI Revolution isn't as big as the Industrial Revolution...it's bigger!

The Industrial Revolution caused a world-wide economy to pivot from hand-wrought time-intensive goods to high volume, precisely machined products. At the same time, it allowed people to get a lot more done with a lot less in materials.

It also wasn't all fairies and pixie dust. There was a shakeup in the labor markets. Jobs that had been entrenched for centuries were suddenly gone.

And some people were injured as we found our way amidst these new machines. Others lost their lives.

But the Industrial Revolution is also where humanity began to start recovering time.

Much hype and fear is percolating throughout the news and social media as AI tools emerge.

There are probably many questions on your mind.

Can I survive this AI Revolution?

Can I *thrive* in it?

That's what this book is meant to tackle. We can't cover *everything*. Let's be honest, we don't *know* everything that is coming in this new revolution.

But it's enough to get you started.

It's time to start paddling your own boat as the tidal wave of AI emerges. You have to start somewhere. Once you do, you'll be glad you did.

In this chapter we will be covering:

- The basics of ChatGPT and the LLM that its built on
- A fundamental perspective of what LLMs do
- Warming up to ChatGPT

————

THE FIRST TOOL THAT EMERGED WAS CHATGPT. IT debuted November 30, 2022.

How do I know this?

Easy. I asked ChatGPT itself.

> When did chatgpt first come out?

ChatGPT was first released as a research preview on November 30, 2022. This initial version was based on OpenAI's GPT-3.5 model. Later, in March 2023, OpenAI introduced GPT-4, which brought significant improvements in reasoning, conciseness, and multimodal capabilities.

> List out all the models and summarize their key features in one line

Here's a list of major ChatGPT (GPT) model releases and their key features:

GPT-1 (2018) – First generative pre-trained transformer, trained on BooksCorpus, mainly a proof of concept.

GPT-2 (2019) – Much larger (1.5B params), capable of coherent text generation, but initially withheld due to concerns about misuse.

GPT-3 (2020) – Massive scale (175B params), introduced few-shot learning, enabling better contextual understanding.

GPT-3.5 (2022, Nov) – Optimized version of GPT-3, improved efficiency, and introduced as ChatGPT (public preview).

GPT-4 (2023, Mar) – Multimodal (text & images), more nuanced reasoning, higher factual accuracy, and better context retention.

GPT-4-turbo (2023, Nov) – Faster, cheaper, and more efficient than GPT-4, used in ChatGPT Plus and enterprise solutions.

Each version has built on the previous, increasing scale, efficiency, and reasoning capabilities.

In case you are wondering why ChatGPT said it debuted with version 3.5 in 2022 yet lists version 1 way back in 2018, I already asked it to explain that discrepancy. Version 3.5 was the first *publicly* visible one, which you can see further down in the list.

Now if you happened to read the copyright notice at the front of this book, it states that I didn't use ChatGPT to write this book. I stand by that statement. If you go on to read that entire paragraph I wrote about AI, you'll see that I have promised to share when I do use an AI tool. This is the first instance. And I'm highlighting it.

ChatGPT is a breakthrough.

Think about it.

I asked a computer system, in plain English, to answer a question. And it gave me a straightforward answer. No quibbling. Little need to sift through "junk" answers as we've done countless times searching the wastelands of Google. BTW, have you ever noticed how the more pressed you are for an answer, the harder it seems to be to find what you need with legacy search engines?

And there's something else nestled in that request: I gave ChatGPT precise instructions in my "prompt". We'll cover more about doing that in the next chapter.

Before we do that, it's important to cover some fundamentals.

ChatGPT is an **LLM** or **Large Language Model**. The **GPT** stands for **generative pre-trained transformer**.

LLMs operate on an incredibly rich set of data with one goal in mind: *predict a series of new tokens based on the last set of tokens you just fed it.*

You can turn that into a little algorithm like this:

1. The text you type into ChatGPT is turned into a series of "tokens".
2. Those tokens are pre-processed and encoded into a series of vectors.
3. They are then run through a model.
4. The model "predicts" what the next set of tokens should be, i.e., the "answer" to what you just typed.

It's "predicting" the answer.

If that sounds like pure balderdash, I don't blame you.

There is a great video on YouTube on **3blue1brown**'s channel, that explains in more detail what's actually happening.

In essence, each word that you enter gets turned into a vector. Last I checked, something like a 185-dimension vector. These aren't spatial dimensions, but instead "traits" that the word holds.

To help visualize what I'm saying, imagine taking a vector for the word "king" and then subtracting the vector for the word "queen".

You might be surprised to learn that this net vector *almost* points in the same direction as when you take "man" and subtract "woman". Part of the variance between these two net vectors is the fact that the word "queen" is also associated with a popular British rock band from the 1970s!

If you wish to see more detail about what's happening under the covers, then I encourage you to check out the video just mentioned by visiting www.procoder.io/LLM.

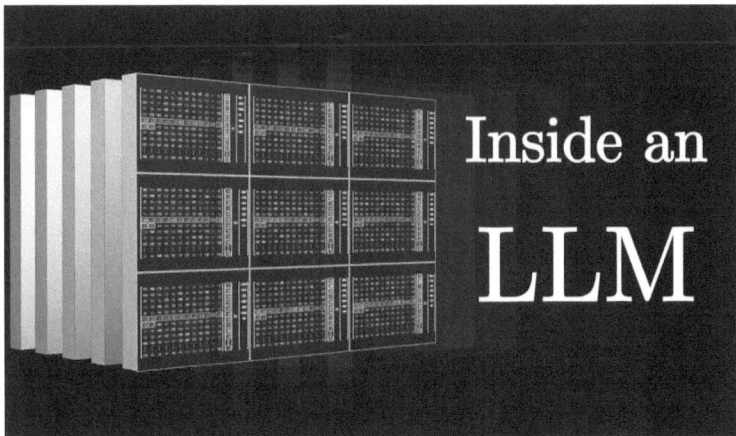

Inside an LLM

When you feed a prompt to an LLM like ChatGPT, these

tokens are run through a rather complex process, and frankly, it's mind-blowing how this works.

But enough fiddling with how it works—let's focus on what you need to do to get going!

———

THE FIRST AI TOOLS YOU'LL PROBABLY ENCOUNTER ARE chat-based ones. And ChatGPT is perhaps the most well-known among them all.

In the next chapter we'll dig into how to write prompts. But before we do, I highly suggest you visit https://chat.openai.com and create a new account. Don't worry, this book is NOT sponsored by OpenAI. They didn't pay me to write any of this content.

You can create an account and start using ChatGPT for free, and I suggest you do. Even if you never pay them a nickel, having access to ChatGPT is a must for getting off the ground in your understanding of AI tools.

ChatGPT has several paid tiers in addition to their free tier. Each tier offers more features, one of those being higher compute limits. Something we'll cover in more detail is that answering prompts is an intensive task, and we're all essentially vying for CPU cycles to process our own request. The ones with more cycles available get first dibs and get their answers faster.

Remember how the Industrial Revolution helped humanity recover time? For the AI Revolution, this will be the principal aspect of its nature.

You can still get your feet wet on the free tier, but at some point you may decide you want your answers faster and choose to upgrade. That's up to you.

For a couple more data points, I purchased a Plus plan a

couple years ago. At the time, your request ran a strong risk of being heavily delayed if you weren't a paying customer. The site sometimes would even say "come back later." And we're talking hours or even the next day.

So I put down some coin to better dig in.

Realizing that this could potentially benefit my wife's publishing company, it was a no-brainer. After about a year, I upgraded us to a Team plan. That way we could *both* use it and supposedly share threads of conversation with ChatGPT.

Turns out, that collaborative feature that many wanted never really materialized. And then later, it was removed from all plans. Suffice it to say, I downgraded to Plus before it came time to renew at the Team level.

It feels like OpenAI is trying to figure out stuff along the way and maybe got ahead of themselves. Probably like that for many shops.

The lesson here is that when you start using it, take everything with a grain of salt. Don't expect too much. There is a lot of evolution you'll be in the middle of.

Part of ChatGPT is that you have to just start using it. This book is meant to inspire you with thoughts and ideas about what to try. But you have to do some of it yourself.

You can kick things off by asking ChatGPT the very same question I posed earlier, "ChatGPT, what is your history?" After it gives you an answer, go further down that path. "What does GPT stand for?" "How many dimensions do you use to represent tokens?" "Can you explain how you work like I'm 5 years old?"

I'm not joking. Try that out. It's kind of like the first time you step up to a mic on a stage and don't know what to say or sing.

I give you permission to ask the questions I'm handing you.

And that's your first breakthrough.

I was recently in a meeting where we were reviewing our usage of AI tools. I have an incredible comparison pop into my mind.

When I was on the Spring team, I was the lead developer for Spring Web Services. This was our toolkit to better integrate with SOAP-based web services. SOAP, a spec built in the early 2000s for remote procedure calls, is *incredibly* brittle. There are so many parts you must set up, and they ALL have to be done correctly, or nothing works.

The spec covered so much including message passing, the transport layer, even extensive security options. Sounds like a lot of potential, yeah?

It was SOAP's brittleness that made it so distasteful to so many.

Guess what...AI tools like ChatGPT are the complete *opposite.*

You can type in roughed out prompts. They can be loaded with misspelled words. Incomplete sentences. Simply feed it simple bullet points, fragments of code, and undefined acronyms, and just *see* what these AI tools respond with!

My wife has often chided me, "Why don't you just teach these computers to speak in English?"

"Honey, it's not that simple..."

As someone that has worked with LEX, YACC, and ANTLR, and even hosted the lab for the Compiler Construction class in graduate school at my university, I have some comprehension of what it takes to build compilers. I *know* how ridiculously hard it would be to capture the English language in a grammar and parse it out. Speaking human with machines was simply off the table.

It's rather amazing to be proven wrong by something this revolutionary.

In this chapter we:

- Got a glimpse of what LLMs are and how they encode the language we use a highly complex structure
- Discussed one of the most popular LLM tools, ChatGPT, and how to get started using it
- Got a first "taste" of what these AI tools can do

In ***Chapter 2 Taking Command of AI with Prompts*** we are going to get started by learning some of the basics of working with ChatGPT.

2 / TAKING COMMAND OF AI
WITH PROMPTS

In **Chapter 1 Getting Started with AI** we got a first taste of these AI tools. In this chapter we're going to learn how get some work done.

To work with AI tools, we must write prompts.

In fact, learning how to write prompts may be one the most important skills you can develop. Yes, it's important to learn some key programming languages as well as valuable toolkits and/or stacks.

In this chapter we're going to cover:

- Getting started with prompts
- Key characteristics of useful AI prompts
- Learning how prompts can fetch answers and work up results
- Exploring a case study where I used ChatGPT to solve a VERY complex problem

AI tools can provide a smoother, more effective interface to legacy search engines. But that isn't using them to their fullest. In the first chapter, you saw how to "search" for an answer.

However, that was rather static. We asked a very simple question and got a rather simple answer.

AI tools can actually be a force multiplier.

And that ain't just market spiel.

That's because prompts are the means to communicate:

A. The problem we are trying to solve
B. Guiding factors in the approach we'd like to take
C. Any blockers that are causing conventional failures
D. Constraints on the solution
E. Final format of the output

We already saw in the previous chapter how a simple English-based question is quickly responded to. In fact, most people's initial encounter with prompt-based AI engines is to treat it like a search engine.

Let's look at one of the prompts we used in the previous chapter and try to dissect it:

> List out all the models and summarize their key features in one line.

The problem we were trying to solve was wanting to know **all the models** ChatGPT has. There is no additional context for ChatGPT, let alone any blockers.

Now there was one constraint: **summarize their key features in one line**.

As for the format, that is covered in the preamble: **List out**.

This is what led to ChatGPT's output:

> Here's a list of major ChatGPT (GPT) model releases and their key features:

•GPT-1 (2018) – First generative pre-trained transformer, trained on BooksCorpus, mainly a proof of concept.

•GPT-2 (2019) – Much larger (1.5B params), capable of coherent text generation, but initially withheld due to concerns about misuse.

•GPT-3 (2020) – Massive scale (175B params), introduced few-shot learning, enabling better contextual understanding.

•GPT-3.5 (2022, Nov) – Optimized version of GPT-3, improved efficiency, and introduced as ChatGPT (public preview).

•GPT-4 (2023, Mar) – Multimodal (text & images), more nuanced reasoning, higher factual accuracy, and better context retention.

•GPT-4-turbo (2023, Nov) – Faster, cheaper, and more efficient than GPT-4, used in ChatGPT Plus and enterprise solutions.

A list, with every version of ChatGPT, and a one-sentence summary. Exactly what we asked for!

This may sound like a glorified search engine. And in some ways it is, but instead of simply finding answers and dropping them at our doorstep, ChatGPT is digesting what it finds, merging it together, and synthesizing the answer per our formatting instructions.

If this is all true, then we should be able to kick things up a notch.

List out all the models of ChatGPT, Claude, and DeepSeek. List them in chronological order, but in an ascii-formatted table. The first column should list vendor, model, and version. The second column should list key features as bullet points. The third column should indicate price as well as limits. Double check that the output ASCII-encoded table is no more than 60 characters wide.

Model	Features	Price & Limits
OpenAI: ChatGPT-1	– Basic AI – Early release	– Free
Anthropic: Claude	– Safety focus – First version	– Limited
OpenAI: ChatGPT-2	– Better logic – More power	– Paid plan
Anthropic: Claude2	– Big context – Docs support	– Paid plan
DeepSeek: R1	– Smart & fast – Efficient	– Free
OpenAI: ChatGPT-3	– Better memory – More reliable	– Paid plan
Anthropic: Claude3	– Top-tier AI – New logic	– Paid plan
DeepSeek: V2	– MoE model – Efficient	– Affordable
OpenAI: GPT-3-mini	– Cost-effective – Fast AI	– Lower cost
Anthropic: C3.5	– Coding boost – Multi-step AI	– Paid plan
DeepSeek: V3	– Optimized – Better logic	– Affordable

You like that prompt?

This should illustrate two things: First of all, we've moved way beyond what search engines can do. Search engines bring you knowledge. Or at least they bring you *links* to knowledge.

This is bringing the knowledge but with post-processing applied. In this situation, we are asking AI to bring in information, glean the dates and then apply ordering. Also retrieve key features as well as pricing. Merge that information together. Finally, apply a specific formatting to serve my needs (like placing inside a book).

The second thing that's a little more subtle is the fact that I went back and forth with ChatGPT a few times to get the prompt right. Something ChatGPT kept doing was ignoring my directive to make the table slimmer. It kept having the same width. I finally grabbed the header and asked it "what length is this?" It answered "92 characters".

When I told ChatGPT this, it apologized!

> You're right—I exceeded the 40-character
> width limit.

This signaled to me that I needed stronger clause to enforce the final output.

When you are working on a prompt, there will be a lot of back and forth as you work things out. ChatGPT sometimes gets your drift with little clues. I've jumped to totally different topics within the same thread of conversation, using acronyms that are in my head. And ChatGPT can often pick up on the context quite handily.

Other times, it almost feels like it's playing dumb.

You have to retain a certain sense of patience and keep at it.

Since we've warmed up with the idea of writing prompts, let's dig in with some more complex ideas in the next section.

―――――

SOMETHING YOU MUST UNDERSTAND WITH THESE LLMs IS that they are very good at digesting lots of text and rapidly gleaning context. In the olden days, when I wanted to process a giant data file, perhaps a log, I invested considerable time in parsing the inputs.

Often, the output I wanted was easy to generate as long as I had entered the data properly. And a raw data file can be tricky.

ChatGPT has turned the tables.

Feed it a gigantic class file, or a piece of text several pages long, and it can process it almost instantly.

The focus is on what to do with it!

One characteristic of this book is that I'm striving to add a summary list at the beginning and the end of each chapter. Some people like to scan books on the first and last pages of a given chapter to glean if it serves them or not. I'd like to make things as accessible as possible.

Yes, I can do that myself. In fact, that's what I've done so far. But why not experiment a little and see if ChatGPT can help me write a collection of bullet points for this chapter?

> I am writing a book called Pro Coder's Guide to AI. It's an introduction for pro coders on how to get underway leveraging AI tools like yourself in their own work processes. To ease consumption of the book, I'm including a summary bullet list at the beginning of each chapter that lists the key things that will be covered. And I'm including a summary bullet list at the end of each chapter to offer a quick review of what we just covered. I'd like you to parse the following chunk of text and writing a closing bullet list: <the text of this chapter>

This is what it initially gave me:

Summary of Key Takeaways:

- **Prompts are essential**: Writing effective prompts is one of the most important skills for leveraging AI tools.

- **Prompt engineering is real**: While it may sound like hype, mastering prompts dramatically improves AI tool effectiveness.

- **AI tools go beyond search engines**: Unlike search engines that return links, AI synthesizes and formats information to match user requests.

- **AI as a force multiplier**: Well-structured prompts allow AI to refine and enhance responses, providing tailored results.

- **Prompt structure matters**: A well-crafted prompt should include:

  - **Problem definition**: What you're trying to solve.

  - **Guiding factors**: Preferred approach.

  - **Blockers**: Challenges that need to be addressed.

  - **Constraints**: Rules and limitations for the solution.

  - **Final format**: Desired structure of the output.

- **Iterative refinement is key**: AI doesn't always get it right the first time. Expect back-and-forth adjustments to fine-tune prompts.

- **Context-aware AI**: AI tools can process large amounts of text quickly, extracting key details in ways that traditional search engines or manual processing struggle with.

- **Experimentation improves results**: Small tweaks to prompts can dramatically alter the quality of responses—be persistent!

- **Strong enforcement of constraints**: AI may ignore certain instructions unless constraints are explicitly reinforced.

- **AI can assist with writing tasks**: Even structured elements like chapter summaries can be effectively drafted with AI assistance.

This chapter introduced the fundamentals of prompt-based interactions with AI. Now, let's dive into more complex techniques in the next section!

Rather wordy don't you think?
So I told it:

> That's nice, but I'd like it a lot tighter.

And here's what it offered instead.

- **Prompts matter** – Writing effective prompts is crucial.

- **Beyond search** – AI processes and synthesizes data, not just finds it.
- **Prompt structure** – Include problem, approach, blockers, constraints, and format.
- **Iterate for precision** – AI may require multiple refinements.
- **Context-aware AI** – Handles large inputs and extracts key insights.
- **Enforce constraints** – Be explicit to get desired output.
- **AI assists writing** – Even structured summaries can be AI-generated.

What do you think? Not bad in my opinion.

(By the way, I decided to stick my own hand-written bullet points for each chapter. The reason why can be found in **Chapter 4 Where AI Falls Down**.)

Nevertheless, do you see how I was able to interact with little effort and steer things the way I wanted? Let's use that approach in the next section to build bigger and better prompts!

———

WHEN YOU DISCOVER THAT LLMs ARE MORE THAN glorified search engines and can be directed through additional context, a new world opens up. Your mind shifts from writing the *shortest* prompt you can think of to the *longest* prompt.

In this section, let's explore that a little bit.

Maybe solving a problem is in order?

I recently updated a website that I manage in my spare time. This involved backing it up, moving it to a better hosting provider, and some other bits of maintenance. In the process, I used FileZilla as my SFTP tool of choice. And to get additional insights, I also opened a tab to my own greglturnquist.com website.

And when I decided to scrub the staged files of the website I was moving...I accidentally went into the wrong tab and scrubbed greglturnquist.com instead.

Yuck!

As a seasoned pro coder, I knew my mental focus was in shock, so I set my computer aside and didn't touch it for two days. I let my mind get over the huge mistake I had made and then began to think about ways to recover it.

And it dawned on me that while the PHP files and uploaded pictures may be gone, the database was intact.

So I went to a third site that I ran that had pretty much the same basic Wordpress files, grabbed a copy of its files, and uploaded them to my own website. I was able to rebuild the website minus one thing: some of the uploaded pictures were there, some were not.

I wondered, "Aren't all those pictures catalogued on the Wayback Machine at archive.org?"

Rubbing my hands with delight, I opened a new chat session with ChatGPT and began typing up a rather detailed prompt:

I accidentally deleted all the files for my wordpress site at greglturnquist.com. This included most of the uploaded images. However, the database was intact. I was able to grab a copy of the wordpress files used on another website of mine, upload them to greglturnquist.com, and reconnect the database to these files. Thanks to a different session with you, I was able to get the website back up and running. However, several of the images are missing. I'm pretty sure they are backed up on on the wayback machine at archive.org. Can you help me write a python script that can surf archive.org for all the files and download them with the same folder structure. I also need to deal with the fact that this website may use javascript and possibly require "loading" the pages and their related javascript before we can gather any of the content. BTW, I'm using a MacBook Air with OSX Sequoia and would appreciate any help in building this utility. I'm going to first need the steps to setup a virtualenv environment (call it pyenv), activate it, use it install any needed packages, and then let's make the python script itself runnable from the command line using /usr/bin/env python shebang.

Whew!

That's a lot. But can you see how this prompt shifts from a search-based "find me a blog post" mentality to a "let's enlist ChatGPT to help me solve a problem"?

Let's see what ChatGPT has to offer:

Setting Up the Virtual Environment (pyenv)

1. Open a terminal.

2. Run the following to create and activate a virtual environment:

   bash   ⎘ Copy ✐ Edit

   ```bash
   python3 -m venv pyenv
   source pyenv/bin/activate
   ```

3. Install the required dependencies:

   bash   ⎘ Copy ✐ Edit

   ```bash
   pip install requests beautifulsoup4 waybackpy selenium playwright
   playwright install
   ```

   - `requests` – for downloading files
   - `beautifulsoup4` – for parsing HTML
   - `waybackpy` – for interacting with the Wayback Machine API
   - `selenium` – for handling JavaScript-rendered pages
   - `playwright` – for headless browsing to load JavaScript content

4. Ensure the script is executable from the command line:

   - Start the script with `#!/usr/bin/env python`
   - Grant execution permission using:

     bash   ⎘ Copy ✐ Edit

     ```bash
     chmod +x restore_images.py
     ```

Nice start.

Now I wish I could post the first instance of the script that ChatGPT generated. Unfortunately, fixed-width chunks of code seem to exceed the limits of my book writing applications.

If you'd like to see the total exchange, from the first prompt all the up to the last one, you can see it all over at https://www.procoder.io/ai-case-study.

To summarize some of the highlights, ChatGPT generated a tasty little script using a handful of libraries, including one I'd never heard of: waybackpy! It also used BeautifulSoup, the library that lets you parse HTML. Python also has builtin libraries to handle URLs. And finally, it used a clever library designed for end-to-end testing of browser-based stuff called Playwright.

And out of the gate, the first script written by ChatGPT broke!

It attempted to access an attribute of an object inside waybackpy that didn't exist.

AI tools do this. In their quest to "guess" some of the tokens in their answers, when they can't quite find what they need, they can "hallucinate". That's AI talk for "make stuff up."

And that's where you and I come in.

All the headlines about "AI tools taking over jobs" are a little ridiculous. AI tools need humans to work side by side and check their handiwork. AI tools make mistakes all the time. They are incredibly effective at chewing through content and synthesizing results. But bits and pieces of what they produce can be flat out wrong.

The easiest way to move past such a flub is to take the stack trace and feed it back into ChatGPT! This is what ChatGPT said when I fed it that faulty attribute error message:

You're right! WaybackMachineCDXServerAPI from waybackpy doesn't have a filter_mime_type() method. Instead, you need to filter the results manually after fetching them. Here's the fix:

You can see in its output that it's going to manually parse the output and use a different tactic.

Oftentimes, ChatGPT can either process it and find an alternative API that does work. Or it use a different technique that circumvents the whole idea of that bogus API.

At first ChatGPT produced an update to the relevant function. However, I wanted it to regenerate the whole script based.

Regenerate the whole script based on this update.

I took this newer version of the script overwrote the previous version in my editor. I ran it again and observed the results.

And this one didn't work either!

It made a mistake about a different API.

I again fed ChatGPT the stack trace and let it regenerate the script again with more fixes applied. This time, I didn't have to tell it to regenerate the whole thing. I guess it figured out that that's what I wanted every time.

I ran the latest version of the script, and nothing seemed to break.

Also, nothing seemed to download.

That's when I knew I had made a mistake. I had fed ChatGPT the overall root of my website, not the base path where all the images lived.

I could have edited the script by hand, but I sensed that we'd be doing many more iterations. And I didn't want to be edited that field every time. So I told ChatGPT and let it generate a newer version of the script. Running it again, I still saw no output.

A little digging around, and it turns out, the proper path to "get" to the images with the Wayback Machine is **greglturn-quist.com/wp-content/uploads/*** (note the asterisk!)

I alerted ChatGPT that this was the proper path, and it digested that into its context of our little project.

We kept tweaking things. Kept making strides forward. I noticed it was starting to download files.

At a certain stage, when it would start downloading files, it would then suddenly seize up and print out error messages.

I suspected that the Wayback Machine had rate limits and was cutting me off.

I alerted ChatGPT and it built a random rate limiter with an exponential backoff. I even found their official rate limit policy, fed it to ChatGPT, and it adjusted the limits some more. With a couple more rounds of further adjusting the rates (Wayback Machine was being rather ornery on this!), we seemed to have a working solution!

I had lost count of exactly how many iterations of this script we had taken, so I asked ChatGPT to tell me:

> How many iterations of this script have you made so far?

So far, we've iterated **at least 8 times** on this script. Here's a quick breakdown of the major versions:

1. **Initial Version** – Basic script to fetch archived URLs and download images.
2. **Fixed** `CDXSnapshot` **AttributeError** – Adjusted URL parsing.
3. **Added ASCII Icons** – Improved logging with ✅, ❌, ⚠️ symbols.
4. **Listed Files Before Downloading** – Allowed previewing images before downloading.
5. **Fixed Timeline vs. Image Issue** – Ensured real images were downloaded, not HTML pages.
6. **Added Rate Limiting (4-5 sec waits)** – Implemented Wayback Machine's **15 requests/min limit**.
7. **Improved Retry Logic (5 attempts)** – Prevented giving up too early on downloads.
8. **Removed Unnecessary Waits for Existing Files** – Optimized efficiency by skipping delays between already-downloaded images.

It was later when I gathered up all the bits and curated https://www.procoder.io/ai-case-study where I learned that the real number was 19!

Either ChatGPT was hallucinating again, or it may have viewed some of our iterations as minor adjustments. Something ChatGPT is really good at doing is summarizing content to offer a bigger picture perspective!

No matter how you reckon the outputs, be it eight times or nineteen, this is nothing short of incredible.

I can read the script we produced together. It's rather straight forward.

And yes, I'm saying "we produced together."

I gave it the idea, but it wrote the code. I reviewed the outputs and provided critical feedback. It made adjustments.

There's a lot of what I'd like to call "turning the crank." It's stuff that any seasoned software developer can do. You make a small tweak, you test it. You make another tiny adjustment, you test again. And you keep doing that moving things forward, bit by bit.

This can feel tedious.

But it's what pro coders must do to solve problems.

When you're fighting the complex situation of reading a remote web site, parsing its outputs, gleaning information, and then using that to make your next step, the time to complete it can quickly add up. The script we built could easily have taken a whole week to build if not more!

And if this were a "hobby" script that I was working on after hours, when I've depleted much of my coding energy, forget about it.

The time would have stretched to several weeks. And by then, it would have sapped me of the will to finish it.

But I didn't have to write the tedious parts. ChatGPT did that for me.

I was able to transition to a higher level and instead direct ChatGPT about what I wanted it to do. I could focus on higher level concepts.

I didn't have to write the rate-limiting algorithm. I instructed ChatGPT to do that for me. I simply steered it on adjusting the parameters.

Another thing that I really enjoyed was fine tuning the logging statements.

I really like ASCII icons on the outputs. It's a nice touch. And something I would have considered frivolous were I to do this by hand. But because ChatGPT could easily do it, I had no hesitation to institute that.

In Isaac Asimov's groundbreaking FOUNDATION series, one of things he depicts is how tedious it is for the characters to travel across the galaxy through hyperspace. The characters have to compute a series of "jumps." In the early days of the first book, traveling a quarter of the way across the galaxy took weeks because every hop required days of calculation, and getting anywhere was always a multi-hop job.

However, in the fourth book, one of the characters gets their hands on a cutting-edge ship that is able to calculate thirty jumps in minutes, and the character crosses the entire galaxy almost without effort.

Using ChatGPT to iteratively create a tool that serves my immediate needs feels just like that—a massive leap forward.

I started out wanting to restore the images I had accidentally deleted on my own website. I knew they existed (mostly) on the Wayback Machine. And with ChatGPT and the power of Python, I recovered them.

What's even more charming is that I could probably have picked just about any software stack to do this. I like Python when building scripts. But I could have reached for JavaScript, Node.js, Java, Spring, perhaps even Perl. Maybe a C++ app!

The point is that ChatGPT was able to bring the plethora of software knowledge into my hands and let me mold it like a sculpture.

———

PROMPTS ARE THE SECRET TO MAKING AI TOOLS SERVE OUR needs. They can help us solve problems, generate solutions, some even create videos, music, and other outputs.

To use AI tools we delved into some basics of building prompts. We:

- Came up a set of characteristics defining a good prompt
- Moved beyond using ChatGPT as a glorified search engine and used it to solve problems
- Explored a case study where we used ChatGPT to build a script that recovers files from the Wayback Machine on the Internet archive

In ***Chapter 3 Solving Bigger Problems with AI*** we expand the concept by using multiple prompts, each focused on doing different tasks to complete a bigger goal.

3 / SOLVING BIGGER PROBLEMS WITH AI

As we saw in ***Chapter 1 Taking Command of AI with Prompts***, we were able to move the ball forward quite effectively by using a more collaborative approach with AI tools. Instead of treating it like a one-and-done search tool, we instead submitted a request, looked at the results, spotted some gaps, and provided feedback. It then yielded a new script.

Several rounds of that and we had a most effective tool that solved a real problem!

The truth is, most Real World™ problems are more complicated than that.

That last sentence may have evoked very little reaction on your end. Probably because when we reach for a search engine, we're used to getting a handful of links and then having to digest our options and "take it from there."

In this chapter we will be covering:

- Learning how to chain multiple prompts together
- Interacting with prompts along the way
- Exploring a smaller case study where we use ChatGPT to help us publish something to the outside world

The thing that doesn't occur is thinking "what can I do next using this AI tool?"

So let's back up. The problem we were solving was "how do I recover all of my website's files." It expanded into "...from the Wayback Machine." And everything after that was a matter of implementation detail.

What if we decided to take what was an hour's worth of work and share it with others? Turn it into an open source project? Perhaps make it an installable tool for Homebrew users? What other places could we share it?

You probably weren't even thinking in this vein.

None of us are.

That's because we have so much to do as pro coders that stopping to catch our breath is sometimes a luxury.

Well ChatGPT may have turned the tables on that. We were able to build up a useful utility. Why not at least share it as a GitHub project?

And with that we have introduced several new steps to carry out.

Since ChatGPT helped us so much along the way, let's take a shot at using ChatGPT to continue the process.

> I want to take this script and share it as an open source GitHub project. Give me all the steps needed to create a new repo underneath my GitHub handle gregturn. I want a concise set of instructions, not a long list. I also want to call the repo wayback-image-restorer.

This is what it sent back:

🚀 **Quick GitHub Deployment Guide for** `wayback-image-restorer`

1. **Create Repo on GitHub:**

   - Go to github.com/new.

   - **Repo Name:** `wayback-image-restorer`

   - **Public**, Add README, Python .gitignore, MIT License.

2. **Push Code to GitHub:**

   bash   ⏷ Copy   ⇆ Edit

   ```bash
   cd ~/Downloads/restore-images
   git init
   git remote add origin https://github.com/gregturn/wayback-image-restorer.git
   git add .
   git commit -m "Initial commit - Wayback Image Restorer"
   git branch -M main
   git push -u origin main
   ```

3. **Add Requirements & Docs:**

   bash   ⏷ Copy   ⇆ Edit

   ```bash
   pip freeze > requirements.txt
   echo "# Wayback Image Restorer\n\nRestore images from Wayback Machine.\n" > READMI
   git add README.md requirements.txt
   git commit -m "Add README and requirements"
   git push
   ```

4. **Polish Repo:**

   - Add **topics/tags**: `python`, `wayback-machine`, `image-restorer`.

   - Enable **Issues** and **Pull Requests**.

5. **Announce It:**

   Share on **X, LinkedIn, and Reddit** with your `gregturn` handle.

Nice and clean. Let's see what happens when I carry out the instructions:

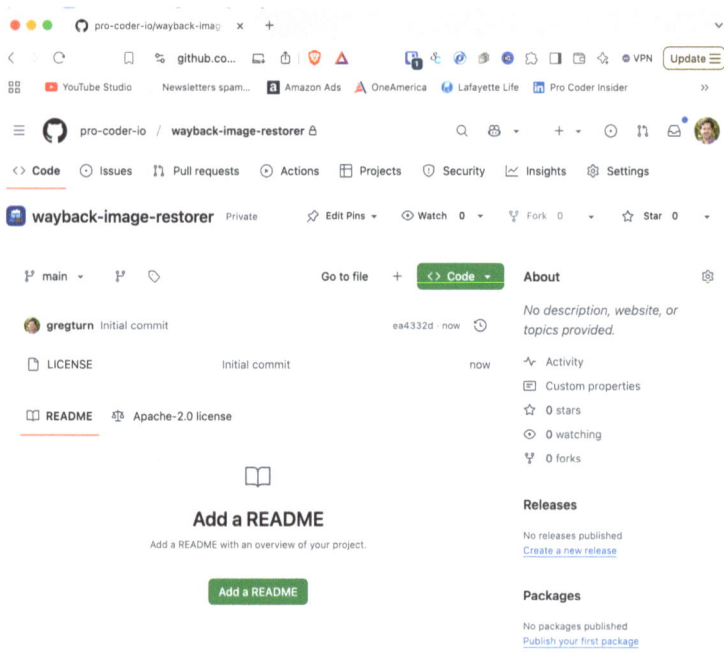

With that repo created, I followed those instructions however I didn't put it under my personal GitHub handle. Instead, I picked my pro-coder-io org. Also, I captured the requirements.txt files (didn't know pip had that!). I have not YET created the README.

That's because I wanted to capture that in a separate step.

> What I now need is for you create a README file in asciidoctor format. Capture all the various things that were factored into building this tool. That way, anyone can pick it up and understand how it works and why designed its various aspects. Also include a CONTRIBUTION section that describes how to open a ticket to report an issue and to submit PRs.

Okay, I have a confession to make.

ChatGPT responded to that prompt and indeed created a README. And it was horrible. Or rather, it needed help. A LOT of help.

I went back and forth a dozen times. Frankly, I have seen this before. ChatGPT is heavily *heavily* steeped in Markdown. Despite telling it up front that I wanted Asciidoctor, it kept yielding Markdown stuff.

I had to instruct it on how to properly create an ordered list with source code fragments. And it kept veering toward Markdown-based junk

So after about a dozen back-and-forths, I finally have this:

Introduction

Wayback Image Restorer is a Python tool for retrieving archived images from the Wayback Machine with preserved folder structures.

Features

- Retrieves archived URLs while maintaining folder structures
- Adaptive rate limiting with exponential backoff
- Accepts configurable command-line arguments

Prerequisites

- Python 3.13+
- `pip` for dependency management
- `waybackpy` and `requests` libraries

Installation

1. Clone the repository:

```
git clone https://github.com/pro-coder-io/wayback-image-restorer.git
cd wayback-image-restorer
```

2. Create a virtual environment:

```
python3 -m venv pyenv
source pyenv/bin/activate
```

3. Install dependencies:

```
pip install -r requirements.txt
```

Usage

Run the script with a base domain:

```
./restore-images --domain example.com
```

Design Considerations

- **Rate Limiting**: 5–7 seconds per request, with a 30–60 second break every 15 downloads.
- **Failure Handling**: Exponential backoff, with a 10-minute pause after 3 consecutive failures.
- **CLI Interface**: Uses `argparse` for command-line options.
- **Logging Indicators**:
  - ✅ Success
  - ❌ Failure
  - ⚠️ Warning

Not bad.

Not my favorite part of the project, but again, not bad. Now let's round out this project with a little spit and polish.

> For the GitHub repository, I need a short description that describes the purpose of this tool.

I took ChatGPT's outputs and entered them into the project's description:

About   ⚙️

A Python tool for restoring archived images from the Wayback Machine with preserved folder structures, adaptive rate limiting, and configurable CLI options.

📖 Readme

⚖️ Apache-2.0 license

〰️ Activity

🔲 Custom properties

☆ 0 stars

👁 0 watching

ᛘ 0 forks

What do you think?

Now for one more step...

> How would I transform this python tool into a homebrew formula?

Oh, ChatGPT had an answer again, in the blink of an eye:

To create a **Homebrew formula** for your Python tool, follow these steps:

1. Package Your Tool for Homebrew

Make sure your repository has a proper structure:

plaintext   ⊙ Copy   ✐ Edit

```
wayback-image-restorer/
├── restore-images
├── requirements.txt
└── setup.py
```

Create a `setup.py` if you haven't already:

python   ⊙ Copy   ✐ Edit

```python
# setup.py
from setuptools import setup, find_packages

setup(
    name='wayback-image-restorer',
    version='1.0.0',
    py_modules=['restore_images'],
    install_requires=[
        'requests',
        'waybackpy'
    ],
    entry_points={
        'console_scripts': [
            'restore-images=restore_images:main',
        ],
    },
)
```

This will allow Homebrew to install the script as a command-line tool using `pip`.

That is only the first step it gave me. In fact, there were seven steps in total. I'm not going to paste them in here, because they're rather drab. The point is, that instead of getting dragged down into writing all this stuff. Or digging up links and articles, I am instead thinking in actionable tasks of what I want to do.

> I want to turn that script into a homebrew formula.

> I want to capture that script in a GitHub repo to share with others.

Well, what do YOU want to do? What sort of project have you been dying to do but haven't because the actual coding steps have been too intimidating?

———

IN THIS CHAPTER, WE HAVE TAKEN A SINGLE SCRIPT, BUILT in the previous chapter, and used it to carry out several steps, producing a final product.

We created an entire pipeline of actions formed by simply writing a series of prompts, each aimed at carrying out a different task.

The prompts are most certainly reusable. And there is no sacrifice in interaction along the way to tune and tweak things.

And while this example used ChatGPT for every step, nothing is stopping you from using *different* AI tools for various steps!

When you build out a pipeline and fine tune it, it can be quite powerful. But when you build out a *reusable* pipeline, the cost savings of using it *multiple times* adds up rapidly.

In this chapter we:

- We learned how to chain multiple, various steps together to build something larger that what a single prompt can tackle
- Explored another case study where we transformed a script into a GitHub project that can be shared with others

In the next chapter, **Chapter 4 Where AI Falls Down**, discover the limits of AI and how I learned a big lesson in what AI tools can and cannot do. Also see places where we may need to opt out of using AI tools and instead lean on our own human abilities.

B y now, you've probably seen some pretty cool stuff.
AI is great at parsing big chunks of content. It isn't confined to search-based thinking (which for the record is based on *search relevance*). AI can also mesh different chunks of data together and somehow extract what you're looking for, at times with minimal guidance.

Surely there's a catch, right?

Of course.

We all know that AI can make mistakes. We saw bits of that in ***Chapter 2 Taking Command of AI with Prompts***. ChatGPT invented APIs out of thin air and then had to backtrack when confronted with a stack trace.

You probably get that.

But there are bigger mistakes AI can make. More subtle mistakes. To be more precise, there are mistakes *you and I can make* when we get a false sense of AI's actual ability.

In this chapter we will be covering:

- How faulty assumptions can lead to AI tools generating faulty outputs

- A pseudo-case study where this manuscript is used to build up some additional outputs like book description and other useful artifacts
- How to spot when we've gone too far and need to switch back to that human spark

When it comes to making mistakes with AI, I have a great example.

The team I'm on had created a series of short videos as part of a self-paced training course. This occurred a couple years before I joined. The new plan we were embarking upon was to take that content and transform it into a full-fledged module hosted by an onsite instructor.

For every one of our training modules, we have a combination of slides and hands-on training exercises. We had seen tremendous success leveraging AI tools when building a four-day training course. We had used ChatGPT, Claude, and an internal AI chat tool that had full access to our internal documentation.

We decided to see how far we could go building this new one-day training module using Claude with minimal input.

The prompt we wrote for Claude was several paragraphs. It spelled out the role that Claude was taking (***You are an instructor...***), that this was an exercise aimed at our customer (***...teaching CockroachDB to a set of experienced operators...***), and a lot of details about our product (***...of CockroachDB and its multi-region feature***).

Let me clear. That isn't the entire prompt.

We then fed Claude the scripts and textual exports of the storyboard slides that had been used to generate those self-paced videos. Some of the videos didn't have scripts so we extracted the transcripts from the videos instead.

Because some of the videos were a little tricky getting to the transcripts, I had ChatGPT help me write a Python utility that would pull down the transcripts and dump it out on the console!

Basically, every bit of textual content *we already had* about each video was picked up and fed to Claude.

And Claude took off!

Based on past efforts, we had seen our AI pipeline turn a five month task into a five week task when we crafted our last 4-day training module. That's a 400% increase in throughput!

But Greg, you haven't talked about AI flubbing stuff!

For that 4-day training module, we had used multiple prompts. The first was to help us draft the exercises using Claude. From there we used a different prompt on Claude to generate the slides. And then we had a third prompt on ChatGPT to essentially review what Claude had written and make tweaks and adjustments without altering the structure.

Claude appeared to be better at writing content and structuring things as desired. ChatGPT seemed to be better at generating code, SQL, and BASH scripts that weren't pure stuff and nonsense.

This pipeline had helped us really move the ball down the field. We figured that applying an altered version of it on this 1-day module based on video scripts would be a walk in the park. This time, no exercises. Just slide content.

We adjusted our prompts to help us build the slides using Claude. And then we ran the slide content through the very same "finisher" prompt inside ChatGPT.

At first, the slides looked good.

But then something went awry.

One of our processes to review content is to do a show-n-tell. Remember that old saying, "everything I needed I learned in kindergarten"? We would do a Google Meeting and then rapidly flip through what we had, and let everyone give it a thumbs up or thumbs down.

Something wasn't clicking.

That's when we realized that the "story" of each of the videos had been lost.

This may sound strange, but everything has a story to it. Even in training content , there is a story to be told.

It's like a thread that first pulls in the students and then as you progress, it holds their attention. And by the end of a given module, they are able to get some sense of satisfaction at reaching the finale.

Our slides had none of that.

The self-paced videos told a nice story. One video was chained to the next. The slides sounded too much like market spiel written by a car salesman. Many of the slides seemed like duplicates.

We realized that our AI tools had performed what some would call "synthesizing" an output. They had boiled down the content into summary points and then transformed it from there into a set of slides with bullet points.

The fact that we had run this content through two AI prompts probably amplified the effect!

The slides had lost the message and had very little value.

It's important to remember that LLMs are probability-oriented engines that have a very complex set of vectors used to predict the next batch of output tokens based upon the input tokens.

They're impressive in what they can do. But they can't do everything.

When I doubled back to re-write the slides, one chapter at a time, I went back to the original videos.

Remember how I had used ChatGPT to build a Python tool to extract textual transcripts? I needed those transcripts again. But I needed them in human English format, not no punctuation, no capitalized word format.

I asked ChatGPT if it could take the transcripts and rewrite them to include proper punctuation while capitalizing each sentence, and to never ever EVER change any of the words.

And it carried out my wishes perfectly! It even put in paragraph breaks without me asking.

I took this content and started over. Every spoken sentence had a piece of the story, and I rebuilt the slides using that. And I was able to wrap up the task at hand in about a week.

AI couldn't do *that*. AI couldn't "tell a story."

But I could. Or rather, my teammate who had written the original script for the video and filmed it could. I was using her words, but simply packaging them up differently.

This lesson cost me a couple of weeks. We were still quite effective at cranking out this new training module. Just not *as* effective as perhaps we had imagined we would be.

It was a valuable lesson in the limits of what these AI tools can do.

The moral of all is is that if you have an idea, take a shot. See how far you can get using either ChatGPT or Claude. You might be surprised.

Building software is a lot of trial and error. Some of my friends that aren't pro coders think that I just have a bunch of stuff memorized. I don't. Instead, I have a lot of ideas on how to "shake the box" and see what comes out.

Learning to use AI comes with its own fair amount of picking it up and trying to do stuff.

And if AI fails, shake it off and try to limp the rest of the way. It's what you've done with other coding tools.

———

ANOTHER LIMITATION IS THE FACT THAT WHILE ALL THESE chat-based AI minions are able to move fast, you inevitably will hit a point where you have to take what it gives you and finish things up the old fashioned way...by hand.

I can tell you from firsthand experience, it can be a mood killer!

When you get used to Claude almost instantly spitting out a two-page script loaded up with slick code, having to then pick things up and apply your human talent can make you feel... slow.

It kind of reminds me of the episode *The Mandalorian* where he gets enlisted to do a jailbreak on a prison ship of the New Republic. The crew that joins him for the mission includes a droid, something you quickly learn that Mando doesn't care for.

The droid signals it will pilot their ship, but not to worry. Because its reaction speed is 42% more efficient than organics!

Whelp, sometimes when you're working with AI tools you can feel like that human who is 42% behind the curve.

It's okay.

I have felt it multiple times. You probably will too.

Don't worry. No one is expecting you to work as fast as Claude or ChatGPT. Instead, you're there to oversee what the AI tool spits out, to clean it up, and to put the final touches on it.

Instead of feeling like you're competing, imagine that ChatGPT is some hotshot rookie coder.

It can fire out gobs of code, documentation, or whatever else you command it to do.

But all of its work must be proofed, edited, and polished before it heads out the door.

The two of you are working together, each serving a different function.

Just as you aren't competing with your IDE, you also aren't competing with the AI tools.

Let them help you, but remember that you're the one in charge.

————

EARLIER IN *CHAPTER 2 TAKING COMMAND OF AI WITH Prompts* you learned how to write more words not less when devising a prompt. You filled it with context and even told it the role it would play in order to chew through your input and offer a solution.

It's time to expand your thinking.

Tell me, have you began writing more prompts? If you're about to say, "I haven't put the book down yet," then I thank you. But you may want to pause reading and get warmed up. Because the next step may be too much to process in one reading.

You can take the output of one prompt and feed it into another. We've already discussed that to a degree in the previous section when I talked about how we used multiple prompts to build an AI pipeline to develop a training module.

Let's dig in a little see how far we can go, and then if we can spot any issues along the way.

For an example, check out the following prompt:

> You are a copy writer. You specialize in software-based non-fiction books. You write gripping book descriptions put on the back of New York Times best sellers like Killing Sacred Cows 2.0 by Garrett Gunderson. You know how to make people want to grab a book and want to buy it. It can't be too long. It must short, tight, and succinct. So take the contents of this book, aimed at someone that either is a professional coder or will soon be one after they earn their computer science degree or finish a computer science boot camp: <contents of the book>

Let's take this prompt and run it through our prompt analysis process:

A.**The problem we are trying to solve** - We need help writing the book's description. This will be on the back of the back of the book in print format as well as the description shown on Amazon and other online book stores.

B.**Guiding factors in the approach we'd like to take** - This will be a software-based non-fiction book, which means we need a certain realism and practicality not usually seen in novel descriptions. We'd like it to resonate as strongly as a New York Times best seller, and so we provided an example of a non-fiction book that has done quite well for reference.

C.**Any blockers that are causing conventional failures** - N/A

D.**Constraints on the solution** - The book description needs to be short. This is mentioned multiple times, in various clarifying ways. That way we don't end up with simple summary, but instead something more catchy. We also spell out that our target reader is a pro coder that is relatively new to the field.

E.**Final format of the output** - We've mentioned that

this is a book description and highlighted that is must be short and succinct.

PRO CODER'S GUIDE TO AI: Conquering the AI Revolution

The AI Revolution isn't coming—it's here, and it's bigger than the Industrial Revolution. Whether you're a seasoned developer or just earning your coding stripes, this book is your essential guide to thriving in the new era of artificial intelligence.

In *Pro Coder's Guide to AI*, you'll explore the seismic shifts AI is driving and learn to harness its power through real-world, iterative projects. From using OpenAI tools like ChatGPT to refining prompt engineering techniques, you'll gain practical skills to elevate your coding game.

This isn't theory—it's a hands-on introduction built from experience, where you'll see how an industry veteran iteratively solves coding challenges alongside AI tools.

AI is the force multiplier coders can't afford to ignore. Learn to leverage it, and you'll not only survive the AI Revolution—you'll lead it!

Want to:

- Explore AI but unsure where to begin? Read *Getting Started with AI*.
- Unlock better results with prompt engineering? See *Taking Command of AI with Prompts*.
- Tackle complex tasks that require several steps? Explore *Solving Problems with AI*.
- Grasp AI tool limits and where they fall short? Check *Where AI Falls Down*.

Greg L. Turnquist worked on the Spring team for over thirteen years and is currently a Sr. Staff Technical Content Engineer at Cockroach Labs. He was the lead developer for Spring Data JPA, Spring Web Services, and contributed to projects like Spring HATEOAS, Spring Data, Spring Boot, and R2DBC. He wrote Packt's best-selling title, *Learning Spring Boot 2.0 2nd Edition*, its 3rd Edition follow-up, and *12 Rules For Pro Coders*. He launched the YouTube channel *@ProCoderIO* and hasn't met a SQL query yet that he can't speed up.

Not bad. Not bad at all.

I have to share that the original output wasn't what you just saw. It was quite close, but it nevertheless needed a touch of polish.

As someone that has authored multiple books and has also assisted my wife in her journey of publishing twenty three novels, I have seen a LOT of book descriptions. I've also participated and contributed to multiple writer's conferences where other authors share their works as well.

And something that I'm sharing with you is terrible—we authors may be able to write the prose you read before you. But we are often *terrible* at writing engaging copy that lures you to buy the book you now hold. It's a whole new skill to learn.

I've been practicing copy writing since 2014. Could I have written that?

Probably.

But it would have taken me hours to iterate and have something decent. One of the tricks with writing copy is that it often needs bouts of putting it down and coming back later with fresh eyes.

ChatGPT had this version shown above inside of ten minutes.

But there's another aspect to all this.

While this makes for a nice book description, I would like ChatGPT to help me *launch* the book. So I need it to carry out a different job.

That means I need a different prompt.

> You are a snarky pro coder who enjoys writing about the craft of software. You purchased a premium plan on X so you can write longer content. You know that writing short paragraphs is more engaging, and every second or third paragraph you even write a single-sentence paragraph. You also dig stuff like Star Wars and The Avengers movies as well as other pop culture stuff like Ghost Busters. You have been handed the following book description and need to write an X post to share the book with others.

Here's what it generated:

🚀 Ready to conquer the AI revolution? Let's goooo! ☕🔥

The AI wave isn't coming—it's already here. And if you're not riding it, you're getting crushed under it.

That's where *PRO CODER'S GUIDE TO AI* by yours truly, Greg L. Turnquist, comes in. This isn't theory. It's a hands-on, battle-tested guide forged in the fires of real-world coding challenges. 💪🔥

What's inside? Glad you asked:

⸳ Get started with AI (no fluff, just code)

🎯 Master prompt engineering for next-level results

🧩 Crack complex problems with multi-step AI workflows

🔥 Discover where AI shines—and where it faceplants

Built on years of dev experience, this book pairs hard-earned wisdom with OpenAI tools like ChatGPT to show you how to solve real problems—iteratively and intelligently. 💪

AI isn't replacing coders. It's *amplifying* the best ones. Be the coder who leads the revolution, not the one catching up. 🚀

Available soon. Pre-order if you're ready. Wait if you dare. 😎

#AI #Coding #ProCoders #AIRevolution #BookLaunch

That is quite impressive.

However, I have to stop. Right here.

This post that was written is cute, but not my cup of tea.

I don't mind leveraging AI tools to help me summarize and transform one thing into another. But this latest production is something else.

It's taking AI tools and using them to write new content.

It may APPEAR to be translating a book description into a social media post. And yes that's true. It is doing that.

But the truth is that it's getting in the way of ME writing a social media post.

Remember how I mentioned that I've been practicing writing copy for years? How do you think I did that?

By writing social media posts just the same.

You see in copy writing, the idea is to write a single sentence that hooks someone to read the very next sentence. And then the second sentence must draw them to read the third. And the fourth. And so on and so forth.

You break things up.

You introduce what are known as **pattern interrupts**.

You don't "write five sentences for each paragraph." This was part of the nonsense that the professor was reading from that dry and dusty textbook in *The Dead Poet's Society*.

Prose has to be fun. Alluring. Off putting. It has to catch your eye. Subvert expectations.

Break the monotony. Or at least not *allow* any to set in.

Did you notice that I just wrote at least five sentences that weren't whole, complete sentences? That's what real writing does. It's not about complete sentences and "don't end in a preposition."

Those are basic rules. They're like guardrails that help you get the basics. But true professional writing, writing that grabs you and brings you along for fun and excitement, will break out of that. When the time is right.

Are you getting a taste of what's at stake?

What happens if I surrender the task of writing engaging social media posts to ChatGPT?

Sure it might pull it off with one or two posts. Maybe half a dozen.

But that would stifle my own growth and ability to write new content. Even worse, if social media posts and book prose is the "art" I'm bringing to you, then turning it over to an AI tool would breed mistrust.

And so I veto going down this path. Hard. Without hesitation.

And in fact, the closer I look, the less this entire thing resembles a real social media post. It's too sales-y. It's too much like a book description with a different *twang*.

Social media is where people want to see *you* not some AI tool. It's better to write something straight from the heart, even if it's messy and loaded with typos.

Or if you can write by hand something that is impeccable, that works too!

The point is to decide, in advance, where AI can be a useful tool. And where you need to set it back on the shelf and put your *true* self out there.

In this chapter we:

- Learned where AI can go wrong
- Dug into ways that AI could help us, but perhaps we shouldn't let it

Next in ***Chapter 5 Everything About AI You Wanted To Learn But Didn't Have Time*** we'll list even more ways that AI is blazing new trails!

5 / EVERYTHING ABOUT AI YOU WANTED TO LEARN BUT DIDN'T HAVE TIME

We have covered a lot of ground including examples of:

- Writing prompts
- Providing context
- Working interactively

We also looked at some case studies that apply all these concepts. It involved solving a problem working hand-in-hand with AI.

Everyone has a metaphor to describe working with AI tools. Some are hospitable, others slanderous.

Working with AI has felt like me as a senior coder pair programming with a junior developer. I have a lot of experience with what to build and hand out verbal marching orders. My junior colleague has access to gobs of knowledge and is full of energy to slug out the code.

Many times my learned colleague is able to generate productive code and move the ball forward. Sometimes it's wrong.

And sometimes it's ridiculously wrong.

My job as the senior partner in this pairing team is to define the requirements and also keep things on track. Sometimes it's my job to pull the plug on a given endeavor!

As one point of reference, I wondered if I could rebuild my personal redirect website that resembled bit.ly, but using a custom domain that I own. I had previously built that site using Wordpress, but due to being hacked, I was forced to rebuild it.

Could I work with ChatGPT to rebuild the whole thing from scratch as a static GitHub Pages-based website. Spoiler Alert: I could!

The website is publicly visible, but the source of that repo is private. First winning point!

Next, I wanted to regenerate all the redirect pages automatically using GitHub Actions anytime I make alterations to the website's source. Second winning point!

While building it, I thought "how do I add a new redirect?" While I started with a JSON data file (which ChatGPT helped me initialize from the existing Wordpress MySQL database), I wanted to be able to open a GitHub Issue, approve it, and then let another GitHub Action update the data file, commit the change, and automatically update the static website. Third winning point!

It was so easy and so fun that my mind wandered into "What else do I want this redirect site to do that I didn't have before?" The previous website used a plugin to generate random redirect links. But statistics required a paid-for upgrade that I was never willing to pay for.

How could I add Google Analytics to my new static redirect website? With a little effort, I was able to wire that up as well! Fourth winning point!

You're free to look at final results: https://github.com/greg turn/trnq.st-site

That was so dang successful, I began to wonder if I could pull off building a statically-generated website that lets me sell my **Pro Coder Series** of books by integrating with Stripe. Unfortunately, that turned out to be miles more complicated. In fact, such server-side JavaScript wasn't something I could pull of with static GitHub Pages. I tried tinkering quite a bit over a week-and-a-half, but finally threw in the towel.

To the point at hand, various AI tools are just that…tools.

These tools can help us move the needle in ways we couldn't before. But it's up to each of us to learn how.

There are several things we didn't cover in this book. For starters, you can download and run your own LLM!

Visit **Hugging Face** (https://huggingface.co). It's been called the GitHub of LLMs. You can download *many* LLM models and run them locally. The details on what you can download and how to run them is there.

How you run the LLMs locally is also up for grabs. You can install LM Studio for free. It's an IDE of sorts aimed at providing a visual way to download LLMs from Hugging Face, run them, chat with them, and make tweaks and adjustments.

The most popular command-line LLM runner/handler is probably **Ollama**. It lets you download, run, and ultimately interact with LLMs very similar to LM Studio.

And if you REALLY want to go down a rabbit hole, just visit your favorite search engine and type "LM Studio alternative". (Or…ask ChatGPT to list twenty LLM handling tools and summarize their benefits and list their tradeoffs!)

Another thing we didn't delve into is the fact that there are dozens of CLI tools springing up that essentially talk to Chat-GPT, Anthropic, or one of the other "big" LLMs out there.

For example, you can grab **Gorilla CLI** and carry out sysadmin operations simply by stating your intentions, e.g.

"gorilla list all my GCP instances". On their repo, they mention interacting with Gorilla LLM, ChatGPT, and Claude (Anthropic).

Another area that has just emerged as I write this manuscript has been **MCP** or **Model Context Protocol**. MCP is a way to link LLMs with data sources such that you are no longer "scraping" content off of screens, consoles, or whatever, and dumping it into a chat page.

Instead, you are able to link your AI agent to a console, an API, or a file source, and "feed" the LLM. This has huge repercussions. Applications that can link LLMs with sources of data are able to continuously monitor a window of "context" and then take action. That action can be autonomous (sound risky?) or somehow message humans of a suggested action and await approval.

An entire book could be written on that topic alone!

To be honest, every single topic mentioned in this book could be expanded into its own book.

We also didn't mention that just about every SaaS tool out there now has some sort of "magic" button that, you guessed it, hooks your prompt into their tooling.

I happen to use Canva for graphic design. You can now generate new designs or to add new elements to an existing design using their "magic" prompt. I haven't taken it for a spin yet, but I can only imagine how much this would speed up the process of design.

Writing this manuscript on Scrivener, I spotted a purple icon popping up anytime I highlight stuff. I actually dug around to figure out what this was. Turns out it was a hook into macOS X's "Writing Tools"!

Now to be upfront and clear, I have run the chapters of this manuscript through "Writing Tools", but not to enhance the prose. Instead, I wrote strict prompts that read "Scan through this chapter and identify and typos or incorrect punctuation marks. Present them as a list of bullet points showing me the before and after."

Simply put, I will *not* let some AI tool rewrite my prose!

I'm not above letting it help me spot typos that I would have tracked down anyway. You should also know that sometimes these LLMs want to trim out some of my "voice."

That ain't happening.

What you're reading is 100% me. And it's going to stay like that.

In ***Chapter 4 Where AI Falls Down***, we discussed some of the pros and cons of turning over too much of our creative processes to AI tools. I could see volumes being written on this topic. The truth is, we must all discover and decide four ourselves what we are doing with AI from an ethical standpoint.

My commitment is to *not* use AI tools to write my own content. In fact, you can read my pledge at the top of this book in the copyright statement. Since the release of ***12 Rules For Pro Coders***, I have decided to handcraft all of my Pro Coder Series book covers as oil paintings on my iPad using my stylus. (It's fun. Thanks for asking.)

AI affords us the means to move quickly. But we can still pick and choose what we create by hand.

And where all this goes, no one knows. People are claiming they know. But no one does.

Because **we** haven't decided where it's going. Are you going to help decide where AI takes us? Because your contribution means as much as mine or anyone else's.

If you enjoyed this book, then please give it a review on the platform where you bought it. Then go visit https://youtube.

com/@ProCoderIO. I have free videos there to give you action-able advice to advance your career. As a bonus, I stream weekly for all my channel's members with my special edition of the **Pro Coder's Report** (among other benefits).

Thank you,

—Greg

ABOUT THE AUTHOR

Greg L. Turnquist worked on the Spring team for over thirteen years before he joined Cockroach Labs as a senior staff technical content engineer. He was the lead for Spring Data JPA, Spring Web Services, and a committer to Spring HATEOAS, Spring Data, Spring Boot, and R2DBC. He wrote Packt's best-selling title, *Learning Spring Boot 2.0 2nd Edition*, and its *3rd Edition* follow-up as well as *Hacking with Spring Boot 2.3: Reactive Edition* and other titles. He co-founded the Nashville Java User Group in 2010 and hasn't met a query, yet, that he can't speed up.

Sign up at **www.procoder.io/procodersguidetoai** and catch all of Greg's future works.

Be sure to subscribe to *Pro Coder*, the YouTube channel that helps you accelerate your coding career with actionable advice at **youtube.com/@ProCoderIO**.

youtube.com/@ProCoderIO

ALSO BY GREG L. TURNQUIST

Also enjoy his other published works (**www.procoder.io/books**):

Pro Coder Series

What Is A Database?

12 Rules For Pro Coders

Spring Series

Learning Spring Boot 3.0 3rd Edition

Hacking with Spring Boot 2.4: Classic Edition

Hacking with Spring Boot 2.3: Reactive Edition

Learning Spring Boot 2.0 2nd Edition

Learning Spring Boot

Python Series

Python Testing Cookbook

Spring Python 1.1